W9-BCL-094

Johann Gutenberg

Master of Modern Printing

Michael Pollard

B L A C K B I R C H   P R E S S ,   I N C .

W O O D B R I D G E ,   C O N N E C T I C U T

Published by Blackbirch Press, Inc.
260 Amity Road
Woodbridge, CT 06525
Web site: http://www.blackbirch.com
e-mail: staff@blackbirch.com

First published in Great Britain as *Scientists Who Have Changed the World* by Exley Publications Ltd., Chalk Hill, Watford, 1992.
© Exley Publications, Ltd., 1992
© Michael Pollard, 1992

10 9 8 7 6 5 4 3 2 1

Photo Credits:
Cover: The Library of Congress; Archiv Fur Kunst: 4, 10, 14, 30, 34, 50, 52; Christie's Colour Library: 45, 48; Exley Photo Library: 55; Explorer Archives: 9 (A Le Toquin), 16 (A Le Toquin), 23 (Bibl. Nat. Paris), 28, 29, 44 (Desmarteau), 49, 54 (Philip Roy); Hulton Picture Company: 7, 33, 38 (top), 43; R.T.H.P.L.: 39; Ronald Sheridan/Ancient Art & Architecture Collection: 5, 13, 27, 37; Ann Ronan Picture Library: 20, 46; Scala: 9, 12, 18, 18-9, 38, 40, 41; Science Photo Library: 51 (J.L. Charmet), 58 (top Malcolm Fielding, Johnson Matthey), 59 (Andzrej Dudzinski); Spectrum Colour Library: 58 (G Mitchell).

Printed in China

Library of Congress Cataloging-in-Publication Data
Pollard, Michael, 1931-
    Johann Gutenberg : master of modern printing / by Michael Pollard. —
        p. cm. — (Giants of science)
Includes index.
    ISBN 1-56711-335-4 (alk. paper)
    1. Gutenberg, Johann, 1397?-1468—Juvenile literature. 2. Printers—Germany—Biography—Juvenile literature. 3. Printing—History—Origin and antecedents—Juvenile literature. [1. Gutenberg, Johann, 1397(?)-1468. 2. Printers. 3. Printing—History.] I. Title. II. Series.
Z126.Z7 P65 2001
686.2' 092—dc21
                           00-012202
                                 CIP
                                  AC

Contents

Awaiting the Decision

Johann Gutenberg, printer, paced up and down his room in Mainz, Germany. He went to the window and looked along the street. He thought he heard footsteps outside, but the sound passed by.

It was late afternoon in November 1455. Several hours earlier, Gutenberg had sent two of his workmen, Heinrich Keffer and Bechtolf von Hanau, to the Mainz city court. There, a case was being heard against Gutenberg, but he could not bear to go himself. In the meantime, he would await word of the decision in his room—a decision that could ruin his entire life.

As he waited, Gutenberg remembered how, as a young man, he had the first thrill of an idea that could change the world. He thought of the long hours, the disappointments and delays when things went wrong, and the constant worries about money. And now, in his mid-fifties, just as things were finally coming together, he might lose everything.

At last, the two workmen came back. He could tell from the way they kept their heads bent, avoiding his eyes, that they were not bringing good news.

"So it is over?" he said.

The two men nodded.

"Have I anything left?"

"Nothing," said Heinrich Keffer. "Johann Fust wins everything—the business, your tools and equipment, all your half-finished work."

Johann Fust was Gutenberg's former partner, the man with whom the printer had shared the most precious secrets of his invention!

Opposite: *This engraving is possibly based on a sketch by one of Gutenberg's colleagues. No formal portrait of Gutenberg has ever been found.*

Below: *This engraving shows a fifteenth century printshop. In the background, compositors are setting type by taking individual letters from a type case. In front, the printer's assistant inks the type surface while the printer checks the printed sheets.*

"But all he knows about is money!"

"Your foreman Peter Schoeffer is to join him. They are to set up a new printing works."

"A new printing works? With my equipment and even my foreman?" Gutenberg was enraged.

"And what about you, Heinrich, and you, Bechtolf? Will you join Fust and Schoeffer?"

The two men looked at the floor again. "We have to live, master," they muttered. Then they left.

The World Before Print

It is almost impossible to imagine a world in which printing—newspapers, magazines, books, maps, leaflets, posters—is not part of everyday life. Yet it was not until the middle of the 1400s that real development in the printing field began. The breakthrough began with a process of movable type. That was a collection of individual blocks, each containing one letter or character. To make a word or sentence, each letter would be placed in a track, alongside the other letters and characters. Though this was a very slow and time-consuming process by modern standards, once it was set up, it allowed many copies to be made relatively quickly.

The fact that there was no printing in the western world until the fifteenth century does not mean that there were no books. Many of the world's great books, including *Beowulf* and Chaucer's *Canterbury Tales,* were written before printing was invented. There were also Latin translations of the Bible and other religious books. The only way of producing more than one copy of these books, however, was to write them out with a quill pen. During the Middle Ages, large numbers of people—mostly monks—were employed as scribes, or book-copiers, for just this purpose.

Royal courts and castles, as well as monasteries, housed large collections of books, all copied by hand on vellum, which was made from stretched animal skin.

A Scribe's Life

Hand-copying was a lengthy task. Someone who ordered a book would have to wait years for it.

Long hours were not the only disadvantage of hand-copying. Bored or sleepy scribes would let their attention wander, or would make mistakes by copying in poor light. Some scribes made their own personal "improvements" to the books they were copying. The result was that many copies of books were "corrupt"—they contained mistakes, passages left out, or extra passages put in. When books were translated as they were being copied— from Latin into English for example—mistakes were even more likely to happen.

The lengthy process of copying of books by hand made the spread of new ideas very slow. During the Middle Ages, a scientist or a philosopher might have developed important new theories—he may even have written a book about them. If he could not afford to have copies made, however, his ideas would live only between the covers of one book and might easily be lost when he died. The result of this lack of printing (and lack of knowledge) was that people were constantly "re-discovering" knowledge. Many worked to solve problems that had already been solved. After printing, knowledge and ideas spread much more quickly. Printing was one of the main factors that created the explosion of ideas known as the Renaissance in the fifteenth and sixteenth centuries.

The First Printers

The true inventors of printing were the Chinese. By the ninth century—six centuries before any Europeans—they were carving complete pages of text onto wooden blocks and were taking copies

Copying books by hand was tedious and time-consuming. This engraving, dated about 1430, shows Jean Mielot, a French monk who was secretary to the Duke of Burgundy, at his copying desk.

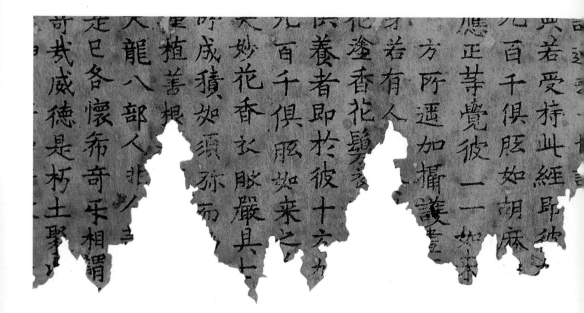

Carved wooden blocks, each carrying a character of the Chinese alphabet, were used in China over 1,000 years ago. This example dates from 975.

from them. Later, they carved letters of the Chinese alphabet onto separate blocks that could be used again and again and in infinite sequences.

Over the course of 600 years, however, the idea of printing did not spread beyond the Chinese Empire. There was very little communication between China and the rest of the world, and the Chinese alphabet is very different from those of Middle Eastern and western civilizations. These factors made the Chinese method hard to adapt for Europeans. Another product of Chinese innovation—paper—had spread to Europe by the eleventh century and was first made in Germany around 1390. The process of papermaking made large-scale printing projects a possibility and was well established by the time Gutenberg began his work.

The Chinese were making paper as early as AD 105. They beat linen rags into a pulp with water, and left the pulp to drain through a wire mesh. The matted threads dried into a sheet of paper.

Left: *Libraries existed before the invention of movable type. Books were either hand-copied or printed from wooden blocks on which both text and illustrations had been carved.*

Above: *Pope Sixtus IV visits the Papal Library in Rome.*

In the seventh century AD, Japanese courtiers were sent to China to learn more about Chinese art and technology. One of the skills they brought back was that of papermaking. This Japanese print shows the Chinese papermaking method, including the process of collecting beaten rags on a perforated screen.

....

"When I get a little money, I buy books; and if any is left, I buy food and clothes."

Desiderius Erasmus
(1465-1536)

....

Hand papermaking took time, but it was quicker than preparing vellum from animal skin. Paper was lighter and more regular in thickness, and it was almost as strong and durable as vellum. It was also much cheaper to produce.

As knowledge of papermaking spread westward, papermakers experimented with new materials. Many types of plants could be used, but one of the most successful was flax. This is the plant from which linen is made. By 1450, paper was taking the place of vellum in most cases.

Keeping Up with Supply and Demand

Just before the Renaissance, there was a "book crisis." The number of churches and monasteries had increased dramatically and each one needed its own copy of the Bible, along with prayer books and books of psalms. Noble families, too, needed books to fill their libraries. In earlier times, a rich family might be judged by the amount of land it owned, or by the number of soldiers it could send to war. During the Renaissance, the mood was changing. Rich people wanted to be seen as cultured and learned, so they aimed to fill their homes with works of art—and with books.

The scribes could not keep up with the demand. The situation must have prompted many people to find a way to produce books faster and more cheaply. There are no written records, but scholars believe that in the Netherlands, Italy, and possibly in France, people unknown to one another worked toward the invention of printing. There was a good reason for them to work in secret: there was no patent law to stop the copying of someone else's invention.

There are two main processes involved in printing. The first is "setting the type"—that is, making up separate letters into words. Those words are made into lines, and are then arranged in page form. The second process is making copies by pressing paper against the type after it is inked. The second process presented no problem, even in the fifteenth century. Presses for fruit—to press apples for cidermaking, for example—were already widely used. They were operated by turning a screw that pressed two blocks of wood together. This idea could easily be adapted to printing.

The Genius of Movable Type

The key to modern printing was the use of movable type—separate pieces of wood or metal for each letter of the alphabet; capitals as well as lower case, each numeral, and each punctuation mark. These could be put together in an almost infinite order to make the text for a few pages of any book. When these pages had been printed, the type could be taken apart and made up again for the next pages. Even for a single page of, say, the Bible, thousands of pieces of type would be needed.

"I was convinced that no wood-engraver would be capable of making wooden types in such a way that they would remain mathematically square."

Charles Enschede, a Dutch engraver who tried to imitate metal type in wood

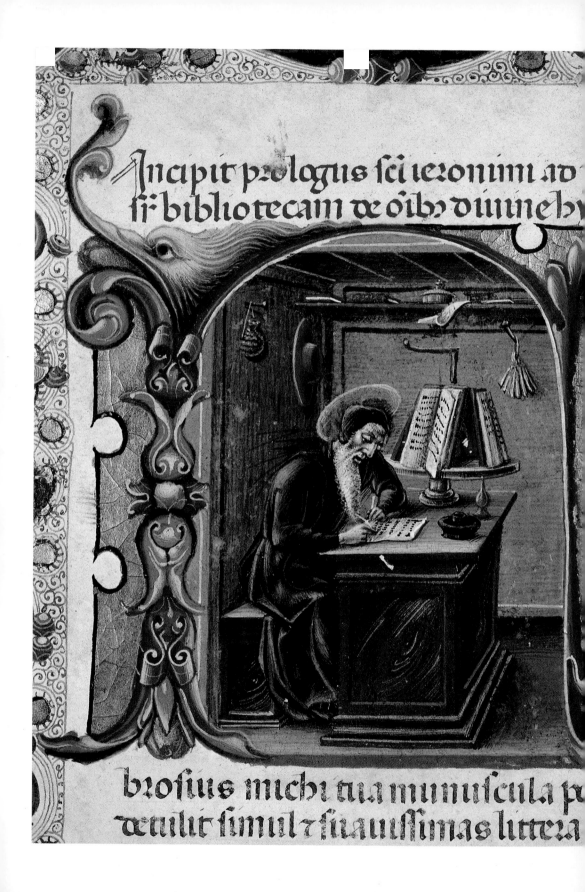

Incipit prologus sci ieronimi ad
sr bibliotecam de oib; diuine hy

brosius michi tua munuscula p
detulit simul et suauissimas litter

They would have to be precision-made so they fit closely together and in line.

Woodcarving was already a highly skilled craft in the 1400s, but there was a high degree of precision needed to produce the small type necessary for the text of a book. That need for precision made it nearly impossible for wooden letters to suffice. Wood is also easily damaged and worn, and does not stay in good condition for very long. A new, more precise and more durable technology was needed.

Who Made Movable Type?

The question of "who got there first" was once a matter of great debate among experts in the history of printing. According to some, a Dutchman named Laurens Coster of Haarlem, was the first to use movable type in 1423. Others claimed that an Italian, Pampilo Castaldi, led the way. Some say that

Above: *A hand-copied book represented months of work and was very valuable. Owners of books often chained them loosely to library shelves so that they could be opened and read, but not taken away.*

Opposite: *Before books were printed, no two copies of the same text were ever exactly alike. Sometimes, scribes would introduce corrections or "improvements" of their own. Extensive decorative work would also be added by the scribe.*

In this portrait of Gutenberg, his fingers seem to be holding a stick into which type would be placed.

Procopius Waldfoghel, a Czech living in Avignon in France, was working on "writing artificially" in 1444. Most scholars, however, now agree that the invention should be credited to Johann Gutenberg of Mainz.

After looking at all the claims and the evidence, experts have decided that it was Gutenberg who first printed a book using movable type. The growth and spread of printing in Europe and on to North America can also be clearly traced back to Gutenberg's work in Mainz, Germany, in the early 1450s.

Mystery Man

Printing was probably the most important development in the history of modern Western civilization. The man who is credited for such a world-shaking invention, Johann Gutenberg, is a figure shrouded in mystery. For long periods of his life, Gutenberg seems to have disappeared—nothing is known of what happened to him in those years. No one knows whether (or where) he went to school, whether (or whom) he married, or exactly when (or where) he was born. The date of his death, February 3, 1468, is almost certain, but he was not considered important enough for his grave to be marked.

Even less would be known about Gutenberg if he had not spent so much of his life involved in court cases. He was involved in a dispute about his father's will, and another about money due to his mother. A woman named Anna took him to court because, she said, he had gone back on his promise to marry her. A shoemaker sued Gutenberg for calling him a liar and a cheat. Almost to the end of his life, Gutenberg was involved in cases against people who owed him, or had lent him, money.

It is mainly from the records of court cases that the story of Johann Gutenberg's life can be pieced together. Although the scene described at the beginning of this book involved some imagination, the court case that resulted in Gutenberg's ruin was real enough. (It is an established fact that Gutenberg sent Heinrich Keffer and Bechtolf von Hanau to hear the court's verdict for him.)

Little is known about Gutenberg's personality, but his frequent appearances in court suggest that he was argumentative and quick to take offense. He was also in financial trouble for most of his life.

Comfortable Beginnings

Johann Gutenberg was probably born in Mainz, around 1398. Mainz, on the banks of the River Rhine in Germany, was a busy trading town. It was also the capital of one of the states that made up the Holy Roman Empire. Its leading citizen was the Archbishop of Mainz, whose rights included the minting of coinage for the state. This activity attracted skilled jewel and metal craftsmen to the city. It also helped to make Mainz famous for jewel accessories, metal-polishing, gold, and silverwork.

Gutenberg's family was quite wealthy. Both his father, Friele, and his uncle were officials at the Archbishop's mint, and it was probably there that Johann first learned the art of precision metalwork. Producing coinage demanded the careful and accurate casting and stamping of gold. It also required an understanding of metals and temperature, the use of casting chambers, dies, and presses.

Because of his family connections, Johann did not have to serve as an apprentice. This meant that he was not tied to the mint when he had finished his training. At the Archbishop's mint, he would have watched as molten gold and silver were poured into casting chambers to make coins. He would have seen how the coins were pressed, cooled, and finally polished. Gutenberg would use this knowledge to develop his movable metal type.

Life in Mainz was not easy. There were constant power struggles between the leading families, and between the families and the Church. When one side gained control of the city, it ordered its enemies to leave. In 1411, Friele Gutenberg was forced to leave Mainz, though his wife and children stayed. In 1428, after Friele's death, Johann moved to Strasbourg, 125 miles (200 kilometers) up the river Rhine. He made Strasbourg his home for about the next twenty years.

Exile

It seems likely that Gutenberg made his living in Strasbourg as a craftsman, and possibly a dealer, in accessories and precious metals. He may have also traded in other goods; in 1439, he paid tax on nearly 528 gallons (2,000 liters) of wine. He was certainly not wealthy enough to have this amount of wine for his own use, so it may have been part of his business.

Some historians believe that Gutenberg could have been using the wine business as a cover for his real interest: experimenting with movable type. Wine cellars provide a convenient place to work undisturbed. The cities along the Rhine were central to the wine trade because the river provided a cheap means of transport. Dealing in wine was an ordinary business in Strasbourg.

While in Strasbourg, Gutenberg started on the experiments that eventually led to his first printed book nearly twenty-five years later. That book—the first printing known to have used Gutenberg's movable type—was a masterpiece of technology. In fact, it was so well produced, so nearly perfect, that scholars are convinced it could not have been Gutenberg's first effort. Judging from the workmanship of this book, the printer had evolved a printing method that remained virtually unchanged for nearly 400 years.

Opposite: *A page from a fifteenth century hand-copied Bible. Decorations on the pages, usually added when the complete text had been finished, provided the scribe with welcome relief from the boredom of copying. They also gave added pleasure to the reader—and increased the value to the book itself.*

• •

"He [Gutenberg] was a man with a ruling passion, and once he had found the channel that gave him at least the reward of achievement, he stayed in it, working out a principle of printing that was to survive unaltered into the nineteenth century."

Sean Jennett, from "Pioneers in Printing"

• •

Women of the fifteenth century were not allowed to benefit from a university education, but the wives and daughters of rich families took advantage of the libraries in convents and family houses.

New inventions do not reach perfection in one step. They require years of trial and error, failure, and endless perseverance. Gutenberg must have gone through all these stages in Strasbourg while he earned a living. Of course, this theory is just the speculation of historians. No trial runs of Gutenberg's printing have ever been found. But that makes perfect sense for a man who was trying to keep his work secret, away from any possible rivals.

Partnership and Panic

There is evidence that something—something mysterious—was going on in Strasbourg. A document drawn up in 1438 offers some compelling evidence.

The document was a partnership agreement between Gutenberg and three Strasbourg men—Hans Riffe, Andres Heilmann, and Andres Dritzehen. As was typical of Gutenberg's affairs, there was eventually a quarrel between him and his partners, which resulted in a 1439 court case. The court records make it possible to piece together some of what Gutenberg was doing in Strasbourg in the 1430s.

It seems that Gutenberg had invented a certain printing process and agreed to teach it to his three partners in return for a fee and loans of large sums of money. What was the secret process? Naturally, it was not described in the agreement, but records mention that some of the money had been used to

This painting of St. Augustine in his study was done in the late fifteenth century, more than 800 years after St. Augustine's death. The study would not have been so well-furnished or spacious, but this shows how a learned man of the fifteenth century would work.

19

buy lead, other metals, and a press. One of the witnesses said that he had lent Gutenberg some money "in connection with printing." This is the first known time that Gutenberg's name is officially linked to printing.

During Christmas in 1438, one of Gutenberg's partners, Andres Dritzehen, died suddenly. When he died, Dritzehen was in possession of a tool, or instrument, that was a vital part of Gutenberg's secret process. After Andres Dritzehen died, Gutenberg sent anxious messages to his house ordering that the mysterious piece of equipment be taken apart. The tool, however, could not be found. Gutenberg also ordered something that he had made to be melted down. If this "something" was type, which seems likely, then Gutenberg must have been in a panic. He was probably asking that Dritzehen's family destroy the results of many years of work.

The process of minting coins, which Gutenberg knew through his family, uses techniques that could also produce type. The impressions on the faces of coins were made by pressing hard metal dies on to "blanks." In printing, pieces of type were made the same way.

The Mystery of the Mirrors

Gutenberg and his three partners seem to have set up yet another dummy business to help conceal their true purpose. In 1439, they planned to journey to the ancient city of Aachen, near the French border. The partners said they had developed a new way of making mirrors, which they planned to sell to the Aachen pilgrims.

This was an unlikely story. Aachen was about 186 miles (300 kilometers) from Strasbourg—too far to make such a business trip worthwhile. There was also no apparent reason why pilgrims should even need mirrors. And there was no mention of ever buying materials to make mirrors. Whatever secret method Gutenberg and his partners were actually devising, no revolutionary way of mirror-making emerged. What did it all mean?

Scholars have come up with one possible answer. There was a popular religious book that had been circulated in hand-copied form for about 300 years. Its title was *The Mirror of Salvation*. This was just the sort of book that pilgrims might like to buy to read on their journey. Could it have been that Gutenberg's "secret process" was not for the making of mirrors, but for making printed copies of *The Mirror of Salvation*?

First Steps

Gutenberg's agreement with Riffe and Heilmann came to an end in 1443. It seems possible, however, that Gutenberg had perfected movable type by that time and had actually started printing. The oldest example of printing from movable type is a scrap of paper with eleven printed lines on each side. The typeface is similar to one that was used by Gutenberg later. Experts have dated it to 1442. An almanac, or star calendar, for 1448, which would have been printed the year before, and a Latin grammar book

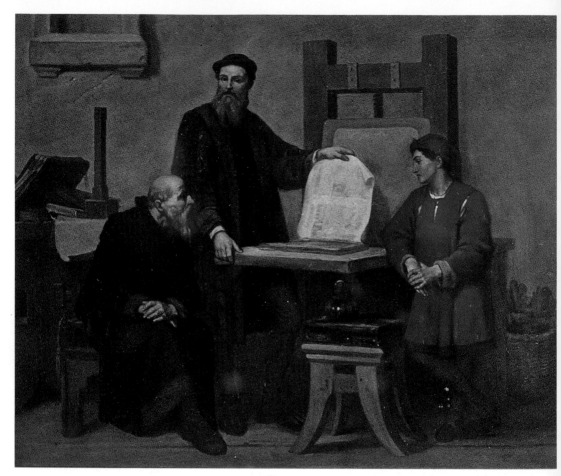

This painting depicts Gutenberg demonstrating his work. He may have done this many times in attempts to interest new financial backers.

have also been traced to Gutenberg, although nothing that he printed had his name on it.

Unlike most of the industries of that time, such as weaving and spinning, printing could not be done at home. Gutenberg would have needed a space large enough to hold presses, stocks of new paper, and printed sheets, with room to dry the printed sheets and collate, or put the pages in order. He would have also needed money to build his presses and make his type, to buy paper and ink, and to pay fifteen to twenty workers. Gutenberg would also need to train workers in the ways of a new industry. This too, took time, patience, and skill.

It is possible that most of Gutenberg's work was in "jobbing"—the printing of small items that are used and then thrown away. A jobbing printer today prints such things as tickets, letterheads, leaflets, and posters. There was no place for these things in fifteenth-century life, but there was a need for something similar called an "indulgence."

Paying for One's Sins

In the fifteenth century, a religious person who had committed a sin could be "forgiven" by paying a sum of money to the Church. In return, he or she would be given a paper saying that the sinner had confessed, was sorry, and had been forgiven. The piece of paper was called an "indulgence." It also acted as a receipt for the money. Indulgences were sold in great numbers—they were one of the church's main sources of money—by "pardoners" who kept some of the money themselves.

By the sixteenth century, it became the rule to have indulgences printed. Because so many more were then available, many more were sold—with huge profits to the church. The corruption in this system worsened and led to the separation of the Protestant and Roman Catholic churches—a movement led by Martin Luther called the Reformation. Scholars know that Gutenberg printed indulgences in Mainz, and it may be that he was doing so as early as the 1440s in Strasbourg.

Early printers took the lettering of the scribes as their models—in many cases it would have taken an expert to tell the difference between a hand-copied indulgence and printed one. If Gutenberg was partnering with a church official (a pardoner) printing indulgences and passing them off as hand-written ones, this business could have yielded a good profit. This theory may explain the secrecy of Gutenberg's printing operation, and the fact that only one small fragment of his Strasbourg work has ever been found.

This is the cover of a hand-copied prayer book from the ninth century. Ivory carvings of scenes from the life of Christ are inlaid into the wood.

Back in Business

Historians are not certain whether, after the partnership agreement ended in 1443, Gutenberg worked alone in Strasbourg or whether he moved back to Mainz. He was certainly back in Mainz by 1448, when he borrowed a large sum of money from a banker there. (The loan, like most of Gutenberg's debts, was never re-paid). The loan was evidently not enough to carry Gutenberg's business forward, and he looked for someone else who would lend him more. His search led him to Johann Fust, a prominent citizen of Mainz.

It is not certain what Fust's primary business was. Some historians of printing describe him as a goldsmith, others as lawyer, others as banker. He certainly had something that Gutenberg did not—a head for business. Whatever Fust's profession was, Gutenberg must have convinced him that printing from movable type was advanced enough to make money. Gutenberg's reputation for being in debt was well-known—his debtors had taken him to court often. Despite the printer's reputation, Fust made Gutenberg a large loan of 400 guilders. They agreed that if Gutenberg failed to repay the money plus interest, Fust would take over his equipment.

Two years later, Fust lent Gutenberg another 400 guilders, although none of this first loan, nor any of the interest on it, had been paid back. This time, Fust protected his money by entering into a partnership. By this time, Gutenberg must have made enough progress to sell Fust on investing more. As it turned out, this was the best investment Fust ever made.

The Breakthrough

During the early 1450s, with Fust's money and his own hard work, Gutenberg perfected a method of casting metal type—and of casting enough type to print his chosen work, the Bible. How did he do it?

In the fifteenth century, coins were made by pouring molten metal into shapes. These shapes would cool into coins called blanks. The blanks were then re-heated, and a die with the coin's design was pressed into each blank. Great pressure was needed to make a good, clear impression. Mints used huge screw presses, which were operated by two men on each arm of the press.

It was logical that Gutenberg, having spent years watching this process in action, should think of adapting metalwork to produce type in a similar way. Adapting the coinmaking process for type production, however, presented Gutenberg with a number of problems.

Only a few different kinds of coins are needed to make up a currency. The United States uses only four main coins. Japan manages with six. To create an upper and lower case alphabet, numerals, and punctuation marks, Gutenberg needed to cast type in more than sixty different shapes. Each shape needed to be as accurate as those for coins, but they also needed to fit precisely alongside all the other characters. Then Gutenberg faced the question of which metals to use. Coins were normally made of gold or silver, with small additions of other metals to make them harder and longer-lasting. Gutenberg, however, needed a metal that was cheap, and that melted easily. Even when he decided on the metal, and purchased it, he could not afford to buy or fuel the huge furnaces that were required to melt the metals.

It must have taken Gutenberg a long time to find solutions to all these problems. The method he eventually devised remained in use for more than 500 years—and this is why Gutenberg is hailed as the inventor of movable type and the master of modern printing.

"A room without books is as a body without a soul."

Lord Avebury, 1834–1913

Casting Type

Gutenberg probably began with the brass punches that German bookbinders used. Each carried a letter of the alphabet reversed from left to right, and was used to stamp the title of a hand-copied book. If a similar punch were used on a bar of softer metal, such as brass, an impression could be indented in the same way. And if the brass was then used as a cast for a still softer metal, such as lead, multiple copies of the original die could be produced. To be truly workable, however, the whole process had to be simple and fast.

Many thousands of characters—letters, punctuation marks, and blank pieces for spaces—would be needed for only a few pages of a book. Each full page of text in an average book, for example, used over 1,800 characters. It has been estimated that 2 pages of Gutenberg's Bible required about 6,000 pieces of type! In addition, the depth of each piece of type had to be exactly the same—if they were different, some letters would print heavily while others would make only a faint mark. The evenness of print in Gutenberg's work shows how incredibly precise his casting work actually was.

The casting process was not only demanding, it was also time-consuming. First, Gutenberg—or a craftsman specially hired for the job—would cut a punch for each character by hand. Then a "proof" or impression was taken from the punch until it was perfect. It would be further checked and improved if necessary with the use of a file or engraving tool. This was important—the die for the letter "a" for example, would be the model for every "a" in many books. When the craftsman was satisfied, the punch would be driven into a piece of brass, leaving an indented impression called the matrix. The matrix, then, was the receptacle for the molten metal (usually lead) that formed the letter part of the type.

"Johann Gutenberg invented printing before the middle of the fifteenth century. Typography is a more correct term, for what he did was to construct the apparatus for making movable metal letters or type and for using these to produce many copies, all alike, of a book."

George Parker Winship, from "Gutenberg to Plantin"

The next task was to create a mold that was accurate enough to make each piece of type exactly the same height. It seems that Gutenberg may have used just one single shape for all of a set—or font—of type, changing the matrix as necessary. This commonality ensured that all characters were the same height. It was necessary to alter the width of that shape, however, to cope with the different widths of letters in the alphabet, for example, "m" and "i." To address this need, Gutenberg made two L-shaped pieces that slid into

In letterpress printing, each piece of type must be cut precisely so it fits tightly to the next. Blank pieces of wood or metal are used to fill spaces. When the type has been set, it is "locked up" in a forme, which prevents it from moving during printing. This illustration comes from an eighteenth century French encyclopedia.

each other and adjusted the space between the characters. In this way, it could be used for any of the letters of the alphabet, or for punctuation marks. Historians believe it was probably an early version of this spacing that "disappeared" at Andres Dritzehen's house, causing Gutenberg so much worry.

The matrix, to form the letter face, was placed in the bottom of this L-shaped casting chamber. Then molten lead was poured in. When the lead was set, the metal could be tapped out as a single piece of cast type. Many copies of that letter were produced before the matrix was replaced with another.

Letter by Letter

The finished pieces of type were stored in cases (the capitals in the "upper case" and the others in the "lower case"). The compositor, or typesetter, then picked out the letters needed to make each word in a sentence. One by one, they were put temporarily into a holder called a "stick." The stick contained both the letters and the blank pieces of type to make the spaces between words. The type was then transferred from the stick and placed on a tray, or galley. The spacing between the lines (today called "leading") was inserted at this stage. When a whole page had been made on the galley, it was placed into a steel or iron frame. Wedges were hammered in at the edges to keep the type firmly in place When the page was made secure in this frame, it was ready for printing. Once it was secure, it was called a "forme" and was ready to be put in the press.

For about 300 years after Gutenberg, the wooden screw press was the only kind in use. The speed of printing was restricted by the time needed to operate the screw downwards, to print, and to release the screw upwards to the paper. Great skill was needed to avoid smudges and achieve just the right amount of pressure between type and paper.

Going to Press

The forme was placed on the wooden printing press, and was secured on the base, which was called the "bed." Printers still refer to "putting a paper to bed," which means taking it to press. The metal type was inked with a leather pad. The printer laid a sheet of paper carefully over the type, and brought down a second block of wood by means of a large screw that had two long arms fitted to it. When the heavy top was lifted, the pressure had caused the paper to make contact with the ink where the metal was raised. Anything lower than the inked surface remained untouched. Once printed, the paper was hung up to dry.

This kind of printing could not be hurried—even the most careful worker surely produced many useless copies ruined by smudges. Yet the quality of Gutenberg's Bible was very high.

Incipit prologus sancti theroni·
presbiteri i parabolas salomonis
ungat epistola quos iungit sacerdon̄·
ium:immo carta non diuidat:quos
xp̄i nectit amor. Comētarios in osee·
amos·z zachariā malachiā·quoqz
pascris. Scripsisse:si licuisset preuali-
tudine. Mittris solacia sumptuum·
notarios nr̄os et librarios sustenca=
ns:ut vobis poτissimū nr̄m desudet
ingeniū. Et ecce ex latere frequēs curba
diuisa posceriū:quasi aut equū sit me
uobis esurietibz alijs laborare:aut
in racione dati et accepti·cuiqz preter
vos obnoxiꝰ sim. Itaqz:longa egroτa
tione fractus·ne penitus hoc anno re-
ticere·z apud vos mutus essem·viduī
opus nomini vr̄o consecraui·interp̄
tatione videlicet triū salomonis vo
luminū:malloth qd̄ hebrei pabolas
uulgata editio pūbia vocat:coeleth·
quē grece ecclastē·latine xcionatorē
possumꝰ dicere:sirasrim·qd̄ i linguā
nr̄am vertit cannicū cannicorz. Fertur et
panaretos·ihsu filij sirach liber·z aliꝰ
pseudographus·qui sapientia salo
monis inscribit.Quorz priore hebra
icum reperi·non ecclastticū ut apud la
tinos:sed pabolas pnotatū. Cui iūcti
erāt ecclastes·et cannicū cannicorz:ut
similitudine salomonis·non solū nu
mero librorū:sed eciā materiaz·gene
re coequaret. Secundus apud hebreos
nusqz est:quia et ipse stilus grecam
eloquentiā redolet:et nonnulli scripto
res veres hūc esse iudei filonis affirmāt.
Sicud ergo iudith z thobie z macha
beorz libros·legit quidē eos ecclesia·sed
inter canonicas scripturas non recipit:
sic z hec duo volumina legat ad edi
ficatione plebis:non ad auctoritatem
ecclasticorz dogmatū affirmandam.

Si cui sane septuaginta interpretum
magis editio placet:habet eā a nobis
olim emēdata. Neqz eni noua sic cu-
dimꝰ:ut vetera destruam9. Et tamē cū
diligētissime legerit:sciat magis nr̄a
scripta intelligi:que non in terciū vas
trāslusa coacuerit:sed statim de prelo
purissime emedata teste:suū sapore ser
uauerit.Incipiūt parabole salomonis
Arābole salomonis
filij dauid regis isr̄l:
ad sciendā sapienti
am z disciplinā:ad
intelligenda verba
prudentie et suscipi
endā eruditione doctrine:iusticiā
et iudiciū z equitatē:ut detur paruulis
astutia:et adolescenti scientia et intel
lectus. Audiens sapiēs sapientior erit:z
intelliges gubernacla possidebit. Ani
aduertet parabolam et interpretatio
nem:verba sapientiū z enigmata eorz.
Timor dn̄i principiū sapientie. Sapien
ciam atqz doctrinam stulti despiciūt.
Audi fili mi disciplinā pris tui et ne
dimittas legem matris tue:ut addatur
gracia capiti tuo:z torques collo tuo.
Fili mi si te lactauerint peccatores:ne ac
quiescas eis. Si dixerint veni nobiscū
insidiemur sanguini·abscodamꝰ redi
culas xtra insontem frustra·degluria
mus eū sicud infernus viuentem z inte
grum·quasi descendentem in lacū:omne
preciosā substantiā reperiem9·implebim9
domus nr̄as spolijs·sortem mitte no
biscum·marsupiū sit unum omniū
nr̄m:fili mi ne ambules cū eis. Prohi
bibe pedem tuū a semitis eorz. Pedes
eni illorz ad malū currūt:z festināt ut
effundant sanguinem. Frustra autem
iacit rete ante oculos pēnatorz. Ipi qz
contra sanguinē suū insidiantur:et

Funded by the loans from Fust, Gutenberg set out to print his masterpiece: the Bible. This may have begun as early as 1450. Most scholars agree that the Gutenberg Bible was certainly underway by 1452. Even with today's high-speed typesetting and presses that can print thousands of pages per hour, this project would be a large undertaking. Using Gutenberg's process, it was a mammoth project—and no money would come in until the job was completed and the Bibles were sold.

The work dragged on. Fust had to provide more money. An account written in 1474 says that Gutenberg was printing 300 sheets a day, using 6 presses. Each Bible was made of 641 sheets, and about 300 copies were produced. With these specifications, printing alone—after the type had been cast—would have taken at least two years.

Scholars believe that, in the middle of production for the 300 copies of the Bible, Gutenberg decided to print more copies than originally planned. This meant going back and re-setting many pages of type, which delayed the completion of the final pages for the 300 copies. This plan may have been the breaking point between Gutenberg and Fust. In 1455, Fust took Gutenberg to court for the return of his money, though the money had been spent and could not be returned. As the court ordered, Fust took over the press, the type, and the completed Bibles—the entire business—in settlement of the debt.

The Gutenberg Bible

The book that Gutenberg and his crew produced is sometimes called the "forty-two-line Bible" because almost all its pages contain forty-two lines in two columns. Each contained 1,282 pages, bound in 2 volumes (the binding was probably done elsewhere). Some copies of the Bible were also sold as separate sheets, for the buyer to bind.

Opposite: *A page from the "forty-two line Bible," Gutenberg's first printed book. For the design of his type, Gutenberg took as his model the lettering used by scribes. This was so successful that some people accused his partner, Fust, of trying to pass off printed Bibles as hand-copied ones to obtain a higher price.*

31

Of the 300 or so copies of the 42-line Bible that were printed, about 40 still exist in museums and libraries around the world. Copies are on display at the New York Public Library in New York City, the British Library in London, and the Gutenberg Museum in Mainz.

The copies are not all exactly the same. In some, large initial capital letters at the start of new chapters were hand-painted, and in others type was used. Experts figure that the Bible was printed in 10 sections, which means Gutenberg must have had enough type to set up about 130 pages at a time. If this is correct, he would have used nearly 400,000 pieces of type—a huge investment of time, metal, and money.

Legal Battles

The period that led up to the dispute between Gutenberg and Fust is the only part of Gutenberg's life that is known in detail. A written account of Fust's accusations against Gutenberg is in the library of Gottingen University in Germany. Fust said that he had originally agreed to lend Gutenberg a sum of money at six percent interest. Later, he doubled that amount, but complained that Gutenberg had paid no interest on either loan. Fust was demanding the return of both loans and the unpaid interest.

The amount at stake, including the interest claimed by Fust, was just over 2,000 guilders. In the fifteenth century, this sum would have bought a heard of about 250 fat cattle. It was a rather large amount of money.

The court ordered Gutenberg to repay Fust's first loan, with interest. Of course, the money had long been spent on metal, paper, and other supplies. The printer was left with no choice but to hand over his type, his presses, and all the work he had in hand. This included all the pages of the forty-two-line Bible, which was nearly complete. Gutenberg would never see a penny of profit from the sale of that Bible.

After the Case

Scholars take sides in the dispute between Gutenberg and Fust. It is natural to sympathize with Gutenberg, whose great work was taken away, but he was an irresponsible debtor. He borrowed money freely without any idea of how he would pay it back. The fact that Gutenberg sent Heinrich Keffer and Bechtolf von Hanau to report back from court suggests that he knew that he would lose the case.

A letter from the Latin Psalter, which was printed by Fust and Schoeffer in 1457. It was produced from metal blocks and printed at the same time as the text.

This engraving shows a typical German court scene in the fifteenth century. Then, as now, courts dealt with business disputes as well as crime.

Regardless of the rights and wrongs of the case, Gutenberg—in his mid-fifties—was left penniless, without his equipment and without work. Fortunately, he was not without friends. Dr. Konrad Homery of Mainz lent him a press and some type, which Gutenberg kept for the rest of his life. Whatever was printed on this press remains undiscovered. Also unknown are details of Gutenberg's last years. Historians do know that, in 1465, Gutenberg was given a pension for being a distinguished citizen of Mainz. He died about three years later.

Inventor in the Shadows

Johann Gutenberg never actually put his name on anything he printed. This has made it difficult for scholars and historians to verify and authenticate much of the work they suspect was Gutenberg's. Unanswered questions and vague circumstances have also aroused much debate about the printer. In addition to the forty-two-line Bible, Gutenberg may have produced a thirty-six-line Bible, a number of other religious books, some Latin grammars, many indulgences, and other disposable material. But it is impossible to be certain. Some of the items that survive seem to have been printed with Gutenberg type but there is no solid proof. In view of how little is known about Gutenberg, it may be surprising that he is universally accepted as the inventor of modern printing.

Gutenberg was first credited as "the inventor of printing" in a book published in Cologne in 1499. At the same time, others were making similar claims for themselves in France, Holland, and Italy. Even if he was not the very first printer to use movable type, it was Gutenberg's system and equipment that led to the development of printing in Europe. Many printers who set up presses in other cities and other countries had been trained by Gutenberg in Mainz.

Printing Takes Hold

After the 1455 court case, Johann Fust found himself in the printing business. He owned all the equipment needed to run it, and a precious stock of Bibles. He may have taken charge of the sale of the Bibles, but he had no practical experience in printing. This explains why he took care to offer Peter Schoeffer, Gutenberg's foreman, a job, and also gave work to a number of Gutenberg's other employees.

Schoeffer was a fine craftsman who continued printing until his death around 1500. Here, the history of printing begins to yield some certainties. Fust and Schoeffer identified some of their work by putting their names on it. They were, in fact, probably the first printers to do so.

The forty-two-line Bible evidently sold well—it probably provided the money for printing Fust and Schoeffer's own book, a book of psalms. It came out in 1457, and was the first book to carry both the date of publication and the name of the printers. It was re-printed again and again, using the same type, until 1516. Fust and Schoeffer were the first printers to store formes of type for future editions. This practice, which later became standard, saved a great deal of time and the expense of re-setting.

During their partnership, which lasted until Fust's death in 1466, he and Schoeffer printed 115 books, including a forty-eight-line Bible. The Fust-Schoeffer rate of production was much higher than Gutenberg's (which was about twelve books per year). A comparison suggests that Gutenberg must have either been very slow, very fussy, or constantly interrupted by technical or financial problems. Some believe this was the cause of his split with Fust.

After Fust's death, Schoeffer continued the printing business. He built it up until it covered virtually the

> "The types of the fifteenth century differed in no essential particular from those of the nineteenth. Ruder and rougher, and less durable they might be, but in substance and form, and in the mechanical principles of their manufacture, they claim kinship with the newest types of our most modern foundry."
>
> Talbot Baines Reed, typefounder

whole of western Europe and included publishing and bookselling as well.

The Age of Print

The lightning speed at which printing spread can be compared to the spread of computer technology during the last half of the twentieth century. The effect that each had on the world is also comparable and equally dramatic. Printing—like the spread of the computer—had some side-effects. The computer streamlined many previously time-consuming tasks—it also put many of people out of a job. So did printing. The victims of modern printing were the scribes, who needed a year to do what a printing press could do in a few days. Some still found work decorating, or "illuminating" printed pages, but soon this too was done by the printer; Schoeffer himself was a pioneer printer of lavishly decorated books.

The printing explosion was accelerated by one major event in the history of Mainz. In 1459, the Archbishop of Mainz died, and two rivals claimed the right to take his place. They declared war on each other, and the citizens of Mainz backed the loser. The winner took his revenge: the new Archbishop ordered all young and fit males to leave the city. This decree affected a number of Fust's and Schoeffer's printers. Gutenberg, who was still alive, was probably excused because of his age. Younger printers hastily made their escape, moving along the rivers Rhine and Main, which meet at Mainz. They set up new printing works at Bamberg, Strasbourg, and Cologne. This set off a chain reaction that "forced" the spread of printing throughout Europe and beyond. Monasteries set up presses that gave work to the idle scribes. Presses became associated with places of learning, such as universities. Other, more commercial presses became large, profitable businesses.

Venice Becomes a Printing Mecca

The art of printing spread at an astonishing pace. Gutenberg's invention was perfectly timed—it released a pent-up demand for books that could not be satisfied. In Rome, Italy, the first press was started by two Germans in 1464. In 1469, another German printer, John Speier, set up his press in Venice. Within ten years, Venice was the world's capital of printing and publishing. There was a plentiful supply of paper in Venice, made in factories that used water from the streams of northern Italy. As the major seaport of southern Europe, Venice was also a good distribution point. Meanwhile, in 1470, the first press in France was

This strange woodcut shows a Death seizing and carrying off printers in a fifteenth-century printshop. The exact meaning of the piece is not known, but it may refer to the dangers and threats many printers faced.

Above: Printers acquired the habit of "signing" their work by using a "colophon" that identified a book as printed by them. This was William Caxton's.

Below: The Vulgate was the first complete translation of the Bible into Latin. Made by St. Jerome in the fourth century AD, it became the standard version used in the Roman Catholic Church. This is the title page of a copy printed in Venice, 1528.

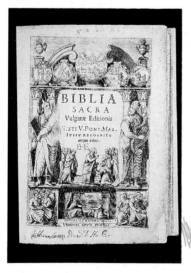

started, followed in 1471 by one in the Netherlands. By 1472, Switzerland had a press running, as did Spain in 1475 and England by 1476.

The World's First English Printer

England's printer—the first printer in English—was William Caxton. He was a wealthy man who took an interest in printing because of his love for literature. Caxton printed about 100 books before his death in 1491. Most of his books were meant to be read for pleasure, which helped them sell well. Thanks to Caxton, people began to see books as a form of entertainment. Reading became something that everyone could enjoy. Soon, reading became one of the "accomplishments" on which well-brought-up noble women prided themselves. Reading aloud to family and guests soon became a popular pastime. Books had emerged from the scholar's study and made their place in the family room and living room.

Fear of Knowledge

It was not long before certain factions saw danger in the spread of books. One powerful enemy of printed books was the Roman Catholic Church. This, of course, was somewhat ironic, since it was printing that spread Bibles and other religious books farther and wider than they had ever been before. Until the fifteenth century, however, learning had been strictly controlled by the Church. There were few schools or universities, and the ones that did exist were Church owned and operated. Church services were sung in Latin, so that only those people educated by the Church would understand them. The Bible, too, was in Latin, and ordinary folk had to trust their priest's word when he told them what it said. In these various ways—before the explosion of printing—the

Church was able to control what people believed, what they thought, and how they lived their lives.

Printing Helps to Spark the Reformation

One of the first major results of printing was that translations of the Bible began to appear in large numbers. The first German translation was printed in Strasbourg in about 1466. It was soon followed by French, Spanish, and Dutch versions. For the first time ever, the Bible could be studied without the guidance of priests. People who read and studied the Bible on their own often became critical of the Church. They noticed, for example, that in its early days Christianity had managed very well without popes and archbishops and all the elaborate and expensive features of the fifteenth century Church. Early Christians had worshiped in simple

buildings, not in richly decorated cathedrals. There was nothing in the Bible about obtaining forgiveness for sins by buying indulgences. Altogether, the picture of Christianity in the New Testament was very different from what the Roman Catholic Church had led people to believe.

Critics of the Church—often writing anonymously to avoid persecution—made full use of the printing press. The ideas they put forward in books and pamphlets played a key role in sparking and then sustaining the Reformation—the breakaway movement that led to the founding of the Protestant churches.

Banned

The Roman Catholic Church hit back. In 1546, it forbade the printing of anonymous books about religion unless they had the approval of the Church. It also published a list of other forbidden books. Anything thought likely to encourage the spread of new religious ideas (which might make people question the teachings of the Church) were banned. The Church decreed that printing or publishing a banned book was heresy—against God and the Church—and punishable by death.

The Protestants—led by German monk Martin Luther—reacted against the all-consuming, oppressive power of the Church. Unlike Roman Catholic services that excluded many, Protestant services were open to everyone. This accessibility appealed to a great many people. New Protestant churches sprouted up throughout Europe, creating a demand for Bibles, prayer books, and hymn books in their own national languages. To answer this demand, many Protestants went into the printing trade. Protestant printers who had been driven out of Britain were among the passengers on the *Mayflower* that carried the Pilgrims to North America in 1620.

Opposite: *Books not approved by the Church were often burned in scenes such as this.*

Below: *A detail from a model of an early Italian printshop. The two printers in the foreground are proof-reading–checking the printed pages for mistakes. The other workman inks a forme of type ready for the press.*

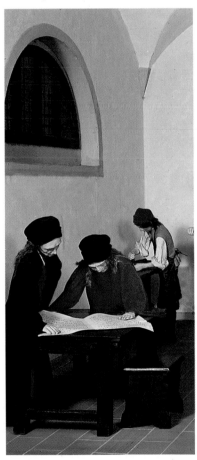

The Pilgrims had a great respect for education. As soon as they had settled in North America, they began to build schools and colleges, each of which required books. In 1638, a press was set up in Cambridge, Massachusetts. Very quickly it was producing the first books printed in what is now the United States. They included books of psalms, school textbooks, and the Bible.

Though they used the power of printing to build a foundation of religious learning, the Protestants also understood the "corrupting" influence that printing could have. From the start in North America, religious books had to be approved by the Protestant Church, and this law was later extended to cover all "books, pamphlets, and other matter." Printing and publishing in the New World did not become free of control until 1730.

The Pilgrims were not the first to take printing across the Atlantic. A century earlier, Roman Catholic priests from Spain had taken a press to Mexico, which was then a Spanish colony. From 1539, this press began to print religious books. Later, following the missionaries of the Roman Catholic Church, a press was set up in Peru. In Central and South America, printing was used not to attack the Church, but to spread its beliefs.

The Politics of News

In 1588, the Spanish Armada (navy) threatened to invade England. News that the Spanish fleet had been sighted was sent across the country by beacon fires. This was unusual. News usually traveled by word of mouth, or by letters between educated people. Many printers tried to meet the demand for printed news, but news often became political—and politics can be dangerous. In 1634, a London man named William Prynne, who published attacks on Charles I of England, had his ears cut off, and spent a year in the

Tower of London. In the eighteenth century, a Cologne newspaper printer who had criticized the government was almost killed by a hired thug. In Berlin, a printer was imprisoned and finally exiled for printing criticism of the government. North America's first newspaper, published in Boston, Massachusetts in 1690, was banned after one issue, though the printer and publisher were not punished.

During the 1600s, some governments began to use printing as a way to get information and orders to the people. Other governments saw danger in the free circulation of news—and, even more, of opinions. Taxes on newspapers, and on the advertisements that helped pay for them, were imposed to discourage their purchase.

All early printing was slow, but the slowest process of all was setting the type. It demanded a large workforce of skilled and literate compositors. In the fifteenth and sixteenth centuries, the ability to read was not common, so compositors were very valuable.

*Governments, alarmed
by books and newspapers
that attacked them, tried
to censor the press. Here,
at the time of the French
Revolution in 1789,
campaigners in Paris
demand freedom to publish.*

Taxes and threats were not the only ways to control what newspapers printed. Writers were sometimes paid by the government to avoid negative information. *The Times of London*, was paid by Prime Minister William Pitt not to attack him.

Chapbooks and Broadsides

Up until about 100 years ago, newspapers were produced mainly for educated men who were interested in politics. The pages contained long columns that reported on speeches and political meetings. There were no pictures. Such papers were of no interest to people who had had little, if any, education. Until the twentieth century, most

women could not vote, so politics and newspapers held little interest to them.

Books, too, were mostly for educated people. They were also too expensive for poor people, and there were no public libraries. This population, though, was eager for their own kind of reading. Printers began producing little booklets of a few pages, with paper covers and woodcut pictures. These were called chapbooks, and they were sold by chapmen or peddlers who went from village to village with such things as cheap toys, needles and thread, and homemade medicines. A chapbook would contain one or two folk tales or Bible stories, with perhaps a nursery rhyme or two. Chapbooks were for the entire family to read.

Broadsides were another popular form of cheap printing. They were crudely printed song sheets that contained only the words of songs. Often, broadsides would suggest a tune to which the words could be sung. Broadsides were also sold by salesmen at fairs and markets.

Some broadsides re-told old stories in verse, but others were about recent events in the news. They were, in a way, the first "newspapers of the people." The subjects of broadsides were similar to what would appear on the front page of a popular news-paper today —crime and punishment, disasters, national events such as a coronation or a war. A big event, such as a battle, would be quickly written up in verse, printed, and rushed out on to the streets. Broadsides on themes like this sold in large num-bers. Lyrics from some of America's most memorable broadsides are still sung today as folksongs.

Guilds

By 1800, printing was a major industry in many cities throughout Europe and North America. Amazingly, printing technology had not changed

As government controls were relaxed in the nineteenth century, a great explosion of printing occurred. Books became cheaper, reaching a wider readership. Women, whose educational opportunities were still restricted, took to reading with great enthusiasm.

The "Illustrated London News," a popular British weekly magazine in the nineteenth century, was famous for large engravings of events in the news. This picture shows a newspaper being printed on a ten-feeder rotary press in 1860.

since Gutenberg's time 300 years before. Printers had concentrated mostly on the art—not the technology—of their trade. Many craftsmen, such as William Caslon, Jean Claude Fournier, John Baskerville, and Benjamin Franklin designed typefaces that were easy to look at and pleasing to the eye. Typefaces based on their designs are still used today.

Gutenberg's method remained in use largely because printers had taken care to protect their trade by forming "guilds." Guilds were similar to modern trade unions. They negotiated rates of pay and hours of work and controlled the training of apprentices. They also supervised the set up of all new printing businesses. Some guilds worked with the government to restrict the number of presses allowed to operate, as well as the number of foundries allowed to cast type.

The guilds had little interest in improving methods of printing. Traditional methods helped to maintain the status quo and kept prices up. The result was that printing became a backward-looking industry. In the eighteenth and nineteenth centuries, printers were quite happy to go on using the methods their fathers had used; satisfaction with the old ways of doing things discouraged the development of new methods. This attitude continued, especially among newspaper printers, until very recently. Printers into the twentieth century fought the introduction of new presses that allowed the high-speed printing of pictures in newspapers. They also resisted the use of computerized machines that did typesetting at lightning speed.

The first technological breakthrough in printing came around 1800 with the replacement of the screw that lowered the press. Instead of screwing the top plate down to make an impression, a lever pressed the block of wood down on to the paper. This was a much quicker operation—the lever went down and was then released so the plate sprang up. The first lever press was built by Earl Stanhope, a British politician and scientist. Stanhope's other inventions included a device for tuning musical instruments and a calculating machine. His was also the first press to be made entirely from iron instead of wood.

Although the lever press was a great improvement, its output was still limited by the speed with which the paper could be placed in position and then removed. It took another German to advance the printing press to its next level.

The Koenig Press

Frederick Koenig was born in Leipzig, Germany, in 1774. In some ways he was similar to Gutenberg. He too had an obsession with printing, particularly

Printing became a valuable means of spreading religious thought. A notable result of printing was that it enabled the texts of holy books such as the Bible and the Koran to be "fixed," freed from errors introduced by scribes.

with finding a way of printing more quickly and with less work. Like Gutenberg, he had no money and depended on finding backers for his ideas.

Koenig had been apprenticed as a printer, but gave up his training to study at the University of Leipzig. By the age of about 30, Koenig was living in Suhl, 93 miles (150 kilometers) from Leipzig, and was running an engineering workshop. By this time, he had made a printing press that worked on a system of pulleys. He traveled through Germany looking for buyers interested in his machine, but was unsuccessful. His search led him to Russia and then to London, where, in 1812, he had a stroke of good luck. He was introduced to John Walter II, the owner and editor of *The Times* newspaper.

London's major newspaper had been prospering for many years. It was helped partly by the war with France, which broke out in 1793, and increased the public's appetite for news.

By 1812, *The Times* was unable to print enough copies to satisfy demand. The only way to increase the output was to buy more presses and have the same type set many times over—a costly process that also meant printing delays. Newspapers depend on the speed of their operations. If they are late with news, their value is lessened. When Koenig demonstrated his latest machine to Walter, which could print over 1,000 sheets an hour, the newspaperman gave him an order for two presses on the spot.

Steam

Koenig's press was a steam-powered printing machine. The forme stayed on the base of the press, or bed. The bed was moved back and forth by steam power—toward the sheet of paper it was printing and then back. This meant that sheets of paper could be put in place and removed without interruption. A roller spread ink on the type, which did away with the slow and messy business of inking by hand with leather pads. Two steam-driven cylinders, taking the place of the top block, then pressed the paper onto the type to make the impression. Koenig's machine needed only two men to operate it—one to feed the blank paper and the other to take the printed sheets away.

The steam presses were installed at *The Times*— or rather, in a building close by—in great secrecy. They were a threat to printers' jobs, and John Walter feared that if his men knew of his plans they would wreck the machines. He had good cause to be worried. His own newspaper had printed stories of hand-loom weavers who had rioted and

Huge national libraries, such as the Bibliotheque Nationale in France and the British Library, grew out of royal book collections. These, along with the Library of Congress in the United States, are the largest libraries in the world.

smashed the new steam-powered looms that were putting them out of work.

So the men from Koenig's workshop were sworn to secrecy. The presses were taken to the building near *The Times* in pieces and assembled by a small group of trusted workmen. Supplies of paper were secretly brought in, and November 29, 1814, was chosen as the day when the steam presses would be used for the first time.

That night, the *Times* printers waited as usual by their hand-presses for the signal from John Walter to start printing. Instead, Walter told them to wait because important war news was on the way and there would have to be changes before the presses started. He had secretly had an extra set of pages made up and smuggled to the new press building.

Despite the relaxation of controls on printing in the nineteenth century, illegal newspapers and books still flourished. This illustration shows a German "underground" press, based in a cellar. Underground presses ran a constant risk of police raids, and often had to move at short notice to new premises.

While the *Times* men waited, Koenig's own staff was running off the next day's paper on the steam press at 1,100 copies per hour. The front page proudly announced to readers that the issue had been printed by steam, "the greatest improvement connected with printing since the discovery of the art itself."

The Next Breakthrough

The output of the new steam press was impressive, but it was still awkward to feed sheets of paper into it one by one. In 1798, a machine for making paper in reels instead of sheets was invented in France. By 1803, reels of paper were being made in Britain. The next step was to develop a press that could take a reel of paper and print continuously on it. In 1865, the first such press was invented by an American, William Bullock, but it proved unreliable.

By the 1850s, the main lines that made up Britain's railway network had been built. The lines made newspaper delivery not only faster, but also more reliable. They also expanded the newspaper's market to places far away from London. During this time, the British government also ended the tax on newspapers. Sales of *The Times* leapt from 40,000 copies a day in 1851 to 70,000 in 1861—and once again the presses were having difficulty in meeting the increased demand.

In 1868, *The Times* installed the first successful presses that printed from reels on both sides of the paper at the same time. Instead of printing from a flat forme, the machine used "stereotypes"—metal plates cast from the type. The curved plates were fitted on to rollers in the press. Once the press was started, it printed continuously, producing a reel of printed paper that was then cut and folded. The rotary press, as it was called, was to become the standard newspaper machine for the next 100 years.

Above: *Early printing used many more processes than those of today. Here, nine printings in different stages were used to produce a full effect.*

Below: *Printing found many uses—this 1892 advertising calendar illustrates the use of gas in the home.*

Typesetting by Machine

The most time-consuming part of the printing process was typesetting by hand. A skilled compositor could set about 1,000 characters per hour—a newspaper could contain hundreds of thousands of characters. While the demand for more books and papers was exploding, publishers still could not produce their products fast enough.

Printers needed a machine that could "justify" the type—that is, produce lines that were all an even length. The hand-compositor did this by "kerning"—adding thin pieces of metal between words and letters until the line was full. Sometimes a typesetter would split long words between lines with the use of a hyphen. All these tricks required a degree of human judgment, and machines could not be taught to think.

The breakthrough came in 1886, this time in the United States. Ottmar Mergenthaler was a German watchmaker who had immigrated to the United States. After eight years of development, Mergenthaler demonstrated his machine to a group of American newspaper owners in the summer of 1886. What he showed them was a mechanized version of the Gutenberg typesetting method.

With Mergenthaler's machine, the operator used a keyboard to assemble a line of type matrixes into which molten metal was poured. This produced a strip of metal type called a "slug," which automatically adjusted to the length the operator had chosen in advance. The slugs were removed when enough had been cast, and they were transferred to the forme. After it was used, the slug metal was melted down and returned to the machine to be used again.

Mergenthaler's machine, christened the Linotype, was the first of a number of similar machines that were to be used in newspaper offices until the early 1980s.

This photo was taken in the composing room of a nine-teenth century printworks.

. . . .

"Hand composition was a real bottleneck in the production of printed matter on a large scale, and there was no newspaper proprietor who was not ready to welcome with open arms a machine that would speed up composition. There was a fortune waiting for the first man to bring out such a machine. Everyone knew it, but no one could produce the goods."

Sean Jennett, from
"Pioneers in Printing"

. . . .

Letter by Letter

Mergenthaler was not alone in working on a mechanized typesetting machine. Another American named Tolbert Lanston, a U.S. government clerk, was thinking along similar lines. Lanston became interested in mechanical typesetting after he had seen a calculating machine that used cards with holes punched in them to control electrical circuits. He thought punched cards could be used to select matrixes for casting type.

The machine Lanston produced was called the Monotype. It was really two machines. The operator sat at a keyboard and tapped out the characters to be set. The keyboard produced a strip of paper tape with holes punched in it—a different arrangement of holes for each character. The tape was then put into a caster. The arrangement of holes determined the position of a small case containing matrixes from which individual type was cast.

It was a race between Mergenthaler and Lanston to see who could perfect their machines and put them on sale first. Mergenthaler won by a year—but in the end, it did not matter. The Linotype was faster, and ideally suited for newspaper work, except that the type it produced was not visually pleasing. This did not worry newspaper readers, who were most interested in the latest news and not how it was represented. Besides, once the paper was read it was thrown away. Books, however, were expected to be pleasing in appearance as well as interesting to read. The Monotype was much better suited to this. So, there was room for both machines.

Despite this steady stream of improvements, the method of producing type was basically the same as Gutenberg's until the middle of the twentieth century—it still involved pouring hot metal into the matrix of the character to be cast. Then, quite suddenly, there was another revolution.

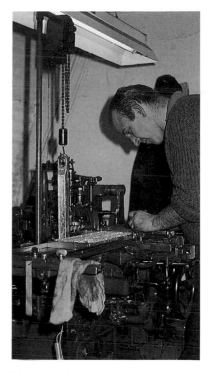

The Monotype casting machine became available a year after the faster Linotype, but it was better suited to books and higher-quality printing. It cast individual letters instead of a whole line of type. Many new type faces were specially designed for use in Monotype machines.

Lithography

Soon after World War II in 1945, a new method of typesetting was introduced. Instead of casting letters in metal, it involved a photographic method of creating images of letters on film. By projecting beams of light through letter shapes cut in a thin sheet of film, this method—called lithography—was ideal for nearly any kind of printing.

Lithography was a radically different way of printing. Gutenberg used letters that stood up, or were raised in "relief." The printing surface with lithography was completely flat. The printing surface, or "plate," was made by shining light through a typeset page onto a photographically sensitive sheet.

Lithographic machines were much faster than old letterpress ones. Setting type photographically, however, was very expensive at first. Much of the

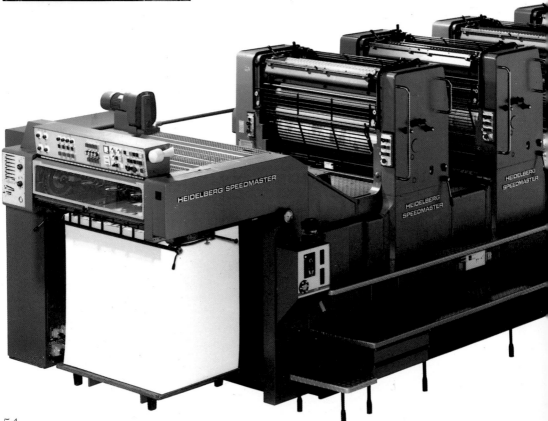

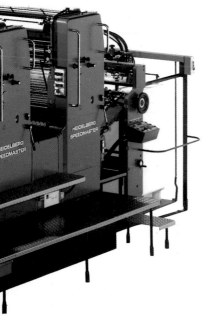

Left: *Rotary presses print from curved plates on cylinders onto a continuous reel of paper. This enables rotary presses to print at very high speeds.*

Above: *The four separate pieces of film—yellow, cyan (blue), magenta, and black—that are needed for four-color printing.*

expense came from the fact that errors could not be spotted until the film—with the entire page's letters on it—had been exposed. This process created difficulties when trying to correct mistakes. Frequently, even the smallest mistake involved resetting the letters. This problem was solved in the 1960s, when computers were used to set type.

Letters that appeared on a computer screen could be seen before printing, so errors could be spotted and corrected before the film of the page was exposed photographically. The computer also streamlined many other tasks, such as changing the design or size of the type. It was also capable of storing vast amounts of recorded information, all of which could be easily recalled on the screen.

Laser Beams

Today, projecting light through letters has been replaced by "digitization." Letters are turned into a code that is sent by laser beams onto film. This method means that many millions of letters can be exposed every hour—light speed compared to the days of metal setting. Even photographs can now be digitized, which means both photos and type can be plated at the same time.

Computers and the advent of digitization have changed the whole face of printing and publishing. It is no longer necessary for every member of a publishing house to be working under the same roof. Work may be done simultaneously on the same publication at various places around the world. Many large daily papers are created and printed in several cities at the same time.

Computerized typesetting, laser beams, and high speed lithographic printing machines have completely replaced all remnants of the original Gutenberg method. Nearly all newspapers, magazines, and most books, are printed today by these

"Just as the invention of writing in early times had helped to 'fix' language in certain ways, spreading common words and ways of using them, so printing further advanced this process. Spellings became more standardized, local words tended to survive only in speech, while printed language increasingly tended to be used over wide areas formerly separated by dialects and local idioms."

J.M. Roberts, from "An Illustrated World History"

new methods. The kind of printing that Gutenberg invented is today only likely to be found at a small jobbing printer, or at a press that specializes in small numbers of handcrafted (and expensive) books.

Reading Explosion!

When Gutenberg's forty-two-line Bible was printed, there were probably a few thousand people in the whole of Europe who could read. Most of them were monks and priests. Instead of reading a book, people learned new skills by watching someone else do them first. They were sometimes entertained by storytellers who had learned their stories by word of mouth from someone else, or had made them up. News was spread by gossip.

Printing changed all that. Apart from religious and political books, educational texts were among the first to be printed in large numbers. Steadily, the range of books became wider. During the first half of the eighteenth century, the first books intended for amusement, rather than the instruction, of children were published. At the same time, the first novels—fiction for adults—appeared.

> "Everywhere I have sought rest and not found it, except sitting in a corner by myself with a little book."
>
> Thomas A. Kempis, 1380-1471

Today, books, magazines, and newspapers are an integral part of daily modern life. They entertain, inform, and help to communicate ideas.

For about 500 years after Johann Gutenberg's death, basic methods of printing remained unchanged. Twentieth-century technology, however, has greatly accelerated the production and improved the quality of print.

Above: *An electronic scanner separates the different films of an original so that they can be etched on to separate plates for printing.*

Right: *A worker in a film house checks quality.*

At first, novels were about the rich—their stories and characters were of little interest to most people. In 1837, Charles Dickens wrote the now famous Oliver Twist, his first big success. This story, about an orphan boy's adventures in London, had a theme and characters that appealed to everyone. The novel, however was not without redeeming social value. It was the first of a long series of Dickens' novels that exposed the cruelty and suffering that many people suffered in their everyday lives.

In the United States, Harriet Beecher Stowe achieved a similar result with her groundbreaking anti-slavery novel, *Uncle Tom's Cabin*, in 1852. Her story exposed the plight of black slaves in America.

Computer technology now enables artists to create images digitally. These images can then be printed and used as the illustrations in a book, magazine, or newspaper. With computer graphics, illustrations can be very complex and visually exciting.

These books, and many others like them, were read all over the world. *Uncle Tom's Cabin* was translated into over twenty languages and became a powerful weapon for the opponents of slavery. Long before movies and television provided a "window on the world," books were exposing the masses to other worlds, other lives, other issues.

Opportunity

With the spread of education in the nineteenth century, reading for pleasure became ever more popular. Books, magazines, and newspapers occupied travelers on rail journeys; bookstalls became a feature of all important railway stations. The advent of gas, and later electric, lighting in the home also boosted the demand for reading material. With improved lighting, reading became less of a strain on the eyes. Publishers brought out editions of classics and popular novels—at very low prices—to feed the public's increasing appetite. Others produced self-education books so those who had missed out at school or college could learn about subjects of interest.

Today, the world bears little resemblance to that of Johann Gutenberg. New methods have taken over the printing and publishing sectors, and a staggering combination of technologies have created an electronic information explosion. Despite the many advances we have seen throughout the centuries, the basic idea to "publish"—to create a system that could reproduce information faster, more effectively, and more accessibly—started with Gutenberg. From his innovation, came the knowledge and information that was needed to build the modern world we enjoy today.

Important Dates

1398	The probable year of Johann Gutenberg's birth in Mainz, Germany.
1428	After the death of his father, Gutenberg moves from Mainz to Strasbourg.
1438	Gutenberg enters into a partnership agreement with Hans Riffe, Andres Heilmann, and Andres Dritzehen to develop a secret process he has invented. Dritzehen dies the same year.
1442	The possible date of the first printed example with Gutenberg's type, a scrap of paper with eleven lines printed on it.
1443	The partnership with Riffe and Heilmann ends.
1448	Gutenberg returns to Mainz.
1450	Gutenberg meets Johann Fust and obtains a large loan from him.
1452	Fust lends more money to Gutenberg. Printing of the forty-two line Bible may have been started during this year.
1455	Fust sues Gutenberg for the return of his money, and takes over the business when Gutenberg cannot repay. Probable year of publication of the forty-two line Bible.
1456	**August 24:** Forty-two line Bible is known to have been published at least some weeks before this date.
1457	Fust and Schoeffer print their first book, a book of the psalms.
1464	Following the spread of printing from Germany, the first Italian printing press, run by two Germans, starts work near Rome.
1468	Gutenberg dies, aged approximately seventy.
1469	John of Speier, a German printer, sets up a press in Venice.
1470	The first printing press is set up in France followed by the Netherlands, Switzerland, and Spain.
1476	William Caxton sets up the first press in England and begins printing books for entertainment. The *Cologne Chronicle* is published which contains the first acknowledgement of Gutenberg as the inventor of movable type.
1529	The English bishops publish a list of banned books.
1539	Jesuit priests introduce printing to Mexico.
1546	The Pope orders that all books about religion must be approved by the Church.
1638	The first American printing press is set up in Cambridge, Massachusetts.
1702	The first daily newspaper, *The Daily Courant,* is published in London.
1703	The first Russian newspaper, *Vedomosti,* appears in St. Petersburg. It is run by the government.
1704	The first American newspaper, *The Boston News-Letter,* appears.

1777	France's first daily newspaper, *Le Journal de Paris,* appears for the first time.
1785	The first issue of *The Daily Universal Register,* later renamed *The Times,* is published in London.
1803	The Town Library opens at Salisbury, Connecticut—the first public library in the world.
1814	**November 29:** *The Times* is printed for the first time on Koenig's steam press.
1820	The first books already bound are published. Previously, buyers had to arrange for their own binding.
1848	**December 29:** *The Times* uses a rotary press for the first time, but it proves to be unreliable.
1858	*The Times* becomes the first newspaper to be printed from stereotypes.
1868	The first successful use of reel-fed rotary presses which prints on both sides of the paper at the same time is achieved.
1886	Ottmar Mergenthaler demonstrates the first Linotype machine to American newspaper owners at the office of *The New York Tribune.*
1887	Tolbert Lanston demonstrates his Monotype typesetting machine for the first time.
1890	The first books with dust-jackets are published.
1982	*The Times* becomes the first national newspaper to be set entirely by photographic typesetting.

For More Information

Books

Fisher, Leonard Everett. *The Printers* (Colonial Craftsmen). Tarrytown, NY: Benchmark Books, 1999.

Graham, Ian S. *Books and Newspapers* (Communications Close-up). Chatham, NJ: Raintree/Steck Vaughn, 2000.

Krensky, Stephen. *Breaking Into Print: Before and After the Invention of the Printing Press.* Boston, MA: Little, Brown and Company, 1996.

Web sites

Gutenberg Homepage
Learn more about Johann Gutenberg and the time he lived—www.gutenberg.de/english.

Robert C. Williams Museum of Papermaking
Find information on papermaking throughout history—www.ipst.edu/amp.

Glossary

Align: To place or set type so that each character is precisely in line with the next.

Baskerville, John: (1706-1775) An English printer for the University of Cambridge, who designed the typeface that bears his name.

Blanks: Pieces of type for the spaces between words.

Broadsides: A popular form of cheaply printed song and tune sheets, sold from about 1650.

Case: The place where each piece of type was stored before use.

Caslon, William: (1692-1766) An English typefounder whose name is attributed to the design made in his foundry.

Cast: To make type from molten metal using the appropriate matrix.

Chapbooks: Small, cheap paper-covered booklets sold in the streets.

Character: Each piece of type, whether a letter or punctuation mark.

Compositor: Person who sets type by hand into a stick, or by machine.

Corrupt: When a manuscript is incorrectly copied by hand so that omissions or additions appear.

Die: An engraving for the casting of type.

Forme: A page of type which has been made secure in a frame and is ready for printing.

Fount: (pronounced font) A set of matching type designed to fit together.

Galley: The tray in which lines of type were stored while the compositor set a whole page.

Illuminate: To decorate the pages of a book with ink, by hand.

Justify: To adjust a line of type to fit a space evenly with no ragged line-ends.

Lowercase: Non-capital letters, so called because of where they were stored in the case.

Matrix: The receptacle for the molten metal which formed the letter part of the type.

Rotary press: A printing press that prints on reels of paper from stereotypes fitted to rollers.

Stereotypes: Metal plates used for printing, made by casting from formes of type.

Stick: The hand-held device into which each piece of type was placed by the compositor. Each single line of text was made up in the stick.

Type: A piece of metal with a raised letter on its upper surface.

Uppercase: Capital letters, named because of the position they were stored in the case.

Vellum: Stretched animal skin that was used for writing on.

Woodcut: The earliest form of book illustration. Simple pictures were drawn on the end grain of blocks of hardwood and parts which were to appear white were carved away.

Index